True

riches

True riches

TODD A. SINELLI

LIT TORCH PUBLISHING

www.littorch.com

true riches
by Todd A. Sinelli

Published by:

LIT TORCH PUBLISHING

PO Box 5264
Santa Cruz, CA 95063
www.littorch.com

Printed in the United States of America

Editors: Alyssa Long and Danny Fitelson
Author Photo: Larry Lapidus
Packaged with: WinePress Publishing

ISBN 1-887357-01-7
Library of Congress Catalog Card Number: 00-191937
First edition, 2001

1 2 3 4 5 6 7 — 07 06 05 04 03 02 01

If I find in myself a desire which no experience in this world can satisfy, the most probable explanation is that I was made for another world.

—C. S. LEWIS

acknowledgments

This book is a compilation and testimony to how God designs us to experience life in community. I am so thankful to all the wonderful people the Lord has placed in my life. First of all, I would like to thank Mike Perkaus. Your wise comments and gracious friendship have encouraged me more than you will ever know. I am eternally grateful. You have been a living example of a life filled with faith and works. Thanks for allowing me to learn through your spiritual eyes.

Thank you to Lance Murdock, who taught me how to be a light in a dark world. Thanks for discipling me at the Chicago Board of Trade and for planting seeds of wisdom that are just beginning to blossom. May my life be a testimony to the fruit of your ministry.

Jeremy Hartman, thanks for your refreshing candor and insistence that I wrestle through these eternal questions to further define my faith and to explain it to others.

Jennifer Showalter, God has given you genius and spiritual eyes. Thanks for sharing these gifts with me. I am richer for knowing you.

Sajit Sasi, thanks for your friendship and prayers. I am blessed to have you as a friend.

Jeff Yelton, thanks for your support and refreshing candor. You are a true man of God.

To all the staff at Mount Hermon, thanks for reminding me that Jesus came so that we may have life and have it to the full. Working with you has been a taste of joy unspeakable. The summer of 1999 will always hold a special place in my heart

My sincerest thanks to Ron Demolar, who offered me a chance to change the world. Thanks for being a man of nobility, character, and love. My life will never be the same after having met you.

To the students of the University of California at Santa Cruz: Your love for God and hunger for righteousness have been fuel in my tank to keep me pressing closer to Jesus. I love you all. This book was written to help steer you toward the greatest teacher who has ever walked this earth. May God bless you beyond what you could ask or imagine.

Last but not least, a big thanks to Alyssa Long and Danny Fitelson. You have been the joyful "thorn in my flesh" as the rough edges of this manuscript have been polished and smoothed through your editing guidance. Alyssa, I promise to never use *towards* again. And Danny, your assistance has made this biggity bomb. May God continue to lead you into paths of righteousness for His name's sake. I could not have done this, nor could I have had so much fun, without you two.

contents

permission

Before we begin, I ask permission to take you on a journey. By reading this book, you will explore your faith, examine your heart, and expand your imagination. We will visit many different perspectives about success, money, work, life, and, most importantly, God.

At times this experience will get a bit uncomfortable. You will be asked to reflect on some tough questions. Once you begin to answer them, I promise that your life will never be the same. *True Riches* will help you consider personal answers to eternal questions.

The first question God asks in the Bible is "Where are you?" I believe this is the first question He also asks all of us. The goal of this book is to assist you in evaluating where you are, where you are traveling, and where you hope to end up.

I invite you to join me on this journey of exploration.

All the best,

Todd Sinelli

introduction
YOUR LIFE—THE FAIRY TALE

Once upon a time, someone had a dream. Cinderella dreamed of romance and of attending the royal ball. Sleeping Beauty dreamed of being kissed by a prince. Even Superman had a dream: to establish "truth, justice, and the American way."

Have you ever considered your dreams? What would you like to do with your life? What would it be like to see your life ending with the "happily ever after" conclusion, the "fairy tale" ending? Wouldn't that be great?

Don't we all want to discover that pot of gold at the end of the rainbow? Some of us dream of marrying a princess or a knight in shining armor. Many of us want to discover the meaning of life. Most importantly, we want to feel significant. We want to feel needed. We want to feel loved. We want to understand what this life is all about.

Winnie the Pooh was once asked his favorite thing to do in the world. Tigger, Piglet, and Eeyore thought for sure that he would answer, "Eating honey." Even Winnie the Pooh initially thought he would say, "Eating honey." The more he reflected on the question, the more he realized that eating honey is great, but it isn't the thing he enjoys most. He told his interviewer that eating honey is wonderful but even better is the moment just *before* he begins to eat the honey. That moment of anticipation is better than the honey itself.[1]

Years ago, if an interviewer had asked me what I thought would make me successful after completing college, I would have answered, "Making money." And make money I did. And lose money. And make money again. I believed that the more money I made, the more successful I would become. As you will learn in this book, God has significantly changed my understanding of success and wealth and the fairy tale.

In this book, we will begin a journey that will show you that a life living for God will culminate in a reward far beyond anything you could ever imagine. Anticipate God's challenge to you throughout this book. Anticipate wrestling with some tough questions. But also anticipate growing stronger because of this journey. If you are holding out for a life with the fairy tale ending, keep reading. If not, keep reading anyway. You may gain a new insight about your place in this world and what it means to live for God versus living for yourself.

This book will focus on how to enjoy true riches. We will look at what it means to be rich. Is it something that we all want and desire? Possibly. We will also explore what prevents some people from living their dreams while others achieve their dreams. What does it mean to be wealthy? Does this life have any meaning? If you have ever pondered these questions, then this book is for you.

Two young boys were playing with what appeared to be shiny rocks on the coast of South Africa. An explorer came by, noticed the rocks, and asked the boys if they would trade them for candy. The boys agreed. What the explorer knew—and the boys did not—was that the shiny stones in their hands were not rocks but diamonds. The explorer took the diamonds back to the United States and made a fortune.

The young boys had held riches in the palms of their hands and had not even known it. What they saw as worthless, someone else saw as immensely valuable. Often we possess things of great value and don't even realize it.

I hope this book can help you realize the precious diamonds you hold in the palms of your own hands. My prayer is for you to discover wealth that you never dreamed possible: wealth defined by God. As the philosopher Benjamin Disraeli said, "The greatest good you can do for another is not just share your riches, but reveal to them their own."

Let us discover what it means to have *True Riches*.

c h a p t e r   o n e

WHAT IS SUCCESS?

"I want you to be a success!"

"Did you hear about Shannon? She is so successful now."

"Michael has really made it."

We hear comments like these all the time. What exactly are these people saying? What does it mean to be successful? To knowingly attain success, it seems as if we must first define this term.

Gerard Smith wrote a book titled *Celebrating Success*. He sought to answer the question, What is success? He asked 150 different people ranging in occupation from professional athletes to princes of countries while including educators, movie stars, and politicians across the world. The responses were fascinating. Each person had his or her own interpretation of success. By many accounts, these people made a lot of money following their passions. Yet not one of the 150 people said making money was their definition for success. Not one.

These are some of the definitions that were shared.

Troy Aikman, a quarterback who led the Dallas Cowboys to three Super Bowls, said, "Success is not so much what we have as it is what we are."[1]

Prince Albert of Monaco said, "Success comes to those who know how to wait."[2]

Actress Rene Russo had a different image of success. She said, "Wisdom is better than rubies or pearls or anything you could wish for."[3]

Performer Pat Boone said success will be standing before God and hearing the words, "Well done, good and faithful servant. Enter into the joys of the Lord."[4]

Debbie Fields, founder of Mrs. Fields Cookies, said, "Success means that you live a legacy that your children can always be proud of."[5]

Each person had a different definition for success. How about you? In your own words, how would you define success?

Success is _____.

After college, I defined success by how much money I could make. This was my target. I really thought that the more money I made, the more successful I would become.

I went to school to learn how to invest and trade in the financial markets. I studied the business world. I learned everything and anything that would help me become a better trader. In college, I majored in business. In graduate school, I received a master's degree in business. After that, I obtained multiple professional designations: Certified Fund Specialist (CFS), Accredited Asset Management Specialist (AAMS), and I also completed the Certified Financial Planner (CFP) program. I continued on to study at The Wharton School's Executive Education Program. I have more degrees than a thermometer.

While in business school, I learned that profits come through one source: investing. In order to generate a profit, you must invest. Throughout our lives we will invest time, talent, and energy in a vast array of activities, people, and places. By applying this insight, I wanted my investments in stock to make me rich. I wrote an eight-year plan for my life when I was twenty-two. One of the things I wanted to do before the age of thirty was to become a millionaire. To be rich was my dream. The surest way I knew how to do that was by investing in the financial markets.

My definition of success has dramatically changed, however, as you will see in the forthcoming chapters.

From a Christian perspective, the main thing to be concerned with is how the Bible—not the world—defines success. The Bible contains answers to questions regarding human nature and human relationships. It is God's instruction book. The Bible explains how we are to live according to God's standards, not human standards. The Psalmist writes, "Your word is a lamp to my feet and a light for my path" (Ps. 119:105). The Bible is our guide on how to live.

Right, wrong, or indifferent, "we must all appear before the judgment seat of Christ, that each one may receive what is due him for the things done while in the body, whether good or bad" (2 Cor. 5:10). God will decide how successful we have been with the time and talents that He has given us.

It's been said that life is God's gift to us. How we live our lives is our gift back to God.

Think about this. Suppose there is an archery competition in town. There are only two participants: you and your neighbor. You are surprised to learn that you are to wear a blindfold and to shoot first. You are blindfolded, and the judge places you into position. You are told to shoot. How well do you think you will do with a blindfold over your eyes? You draw an arrow and end up missing the target by more than fifty feet. The crowd is amused.

While you are still wearing the blindfold, your neighbor begins. You hear her walk into position. You also hear her coach herself as she prepares to launch an arrow. "Take aim, focus on the target, see the center, and release." Brief pause. "Bull's-eye!"

She then walks up to you, sarcastically takes off your blindfold, and says, "It's all about focusing on the target."[6]

Why am I sharing what seems to be a ridiculous story? Because we are considering success. We must aim for success as if aiming for a target. We must be able to see a bull's-eye to know if we hit it or not. If we are not aiming for something, our lives will travel like stray arrows. We will never know if we have hit the bull's-eye because we have never even pictured the target.

What major targets are you aiming at in your life? Could you narrow it down to one?

In the movie *City Slickers,* there is a scene in which Jack Palance and Billy Crystal are riding horses through the desert. Palance, as the rough and rugged cowboy Curly, asks Crystal, playing Mitch, if he knows the secret of life.

Mitch replies, "No, what is it?"

Curly stops his horse, looks deeply at Mitch, lifts one finger, and says, "This."

"Your finger?" asks Mitch. "That is the meaning of life?"

Curly again raises his finger and says, "One thing. Just one thing. You stick to that and everything else don't mean squat."

Mitch then wants to know, "What is the one thing?"

Curly responds, "That is for you to find out."[7]

Doesn't everyone want to find that one thing that will give his or her life meaning? Could the secret of life be centered on one thing?

Silly? Profound? Insightful? This scene from *City Slickers* may be all of these. Yet, we all need to discover our own "one thing" that gets us excited about being alive.

Think about where you spend your time. What do you do most of the day? What thoughts fill your head? Where are you focusing your attention?

I ask again, What is success? What is your definition? Consider the words that motivate Pat Boone. Success for him will be standing before God and hearing the words, "Well done, good and faithful servant."

Each day we are presented with choices. We may choose to work or play, to take risks or use extreme caution. We can choose to become artists, athletes, teachers, doctors, or company executives. Life is a balance between defining what we want and realizing what must be done to achieve it.

We can choose to go through life in a state of fear, fearing whether or not we will ever have enough money or enough friends, fearing criticism, fearing rejection. But why would we let fear stand in the way of living a life filled with adventure? Why don't we choose a life full of courage? Courageously taking risks. Courageously getting educated. Courageously following our dreams. We need courage. Courage to risk loving too much. Courage to live a life of faith. And the courage to live a life committed to following God.

Envision how the world could become better. Now see yourself as the change that you want to see in this world. Is your dream to educate the youth, paint beautiful art, feed the homeless? Or is your dream to become a musician, business leader, or professional athlete?

Live a life using the unique gifts and talents that God has bestowed upon you, then give Him the credit. Psalm 115:1 says, "Not to us, O LORD, not to us but to your name be the glory, because of your love and faithfulness." God gives us many opportunities to serve Him and become humble servants that live to honor His name.

In my opinion, having a great job would be nice. To have a wonderful family and a wife that loves me would be great. To travel around the world inspiring others to follow God would also bring joy to my heart. But, the only thing that I live for is to live a life pleasing to God. That is what I use to define my success. I want to love Jesus with all my heart, all my soul, and all my mind. My success will come when I stand before the Lord and hear, "Well done, good and faithful servant!" (Matt. 25:21).

Ultimately my complete success rests not on the basis of how successful I am in the eyes of the world but on how faithful I have been in the situations God has placed me.

Success is not about the money you make. It's not about fame. Nor is it about building your own empire. Consider the words of Christian psychologist Dr. James Dobson:

> I have concluded that the accumulation of wealth, even if I could achieve it, is an insufficient reason for living. When I reach the end of my days, a moment or two from now, I must look backward on something more meaningful than the pursuit of houses and land and machines and stocks and bonds. Nor is fame of any lasting benefit. I will consider my earthly existence to have been wasted unless I can recall a loving family, a consistent investment

21

in the lives of people, and an earnest attempt to serve the God who made me. Nothing else makes much sense.[8]

Please don't misunderstand me. I don't think that making a lot of money is bad. As a matter of fact, I am elated when I see people making large amounts of money. Money and the ability to create wealth can be a fantastic gift from God. As the Bible states, "You may say to yourself, 'My power and the strength of my hands have produced this wealth for me.' But remember the LORD your God, for it is he who gives you the ability to produce wealth, and so confirms his covenant, which he swore to your forefathers, as it is today" (Deut. 8:17–18). Each time I see people making enormous amounts of money, my immediate prayer for them is that God will allow them to enjoy every dime that they have been given. I believe, however, just as all the people interviewed in Smith's book, that money is not the correct definition of success.

Remember, life is God's gift to you. How you live your life is your gift back to God.

Once you define success and what it is that you want from life, then you can live for your "one thing." Once you discover what you want more than anything else, you will have found your heart's desire.

I believe the ultimate definition of success is living a life that is pleasing to God. Be a success in God's eyes. Live for His glory. As Dr. Dobson mentioned, "Nothing else makes much sense."

But what happens if God does bless us with financial abundance? What should we do if financial success comes our way? What will we do with our money and how can we use it to honor God?

Let us look at what the Bible says about money.

HOW TO ALWAYS BE RICH

o you know what subject Jesus discussed the most in the Bible? Here is a hint: He talked more about this topic than the topic of heaven. He talked more about this than He spoke about prayer. Is faith, sin, or His second coming the answer? No. The topic Jesus discussed the most was money. Surprising, isn't it?

John MacArthur from Grace Community Church in Panorama City, California shares that "Sixteen out of thirty-eight of Christ's parables deal with money. More is said in the New Testament about money than is said about heaven and hell combined. Five times more is said about money than prayer; and while there are five hundred plus verses on both prayer and faith, there are over two thousand verses dealing with money and possessions."[1]

The point is that God has a lot to say about money.

Wealth. Riches. Money. These topics have endured through time. At some point in our lives we will ask, "What is wealth? What does it mean to be rich?" It is an inevitable discussion. The news, entertainment, and many of our conversations are filled with this topic.

"That person is rich!"

"She's loaded."

"He has tons of money."

We hear these expressions often. Yet do they define wealth? Who is to say that someone is or is not rich? What does it mean to be rich?

Anthony Robbins, a motivational speaker, conducted a wealth mastery retreat in which he asked all of his guests the same question: "What is your definition of being rich?" This gathering consisted of some of the richest people in the United States. Their answers varied. Some of the guests said having a personal airplane constitutes being rich. One guest responded that having a house on every continent is the sign of being rich. Another said having millions of dollars is the definition of wealth. Others said that not ever having to ask how much something costs is the mark of being wealthy.

For many years, I bought into some of the same thinking. The movie *Wall Street* had a dramatic impact on my life as a young man. After seeing that movie in 1990, I knew without a shadow of doubt that I was headed for life in the financial markets. There was a scene in the movie where Gordon Gecko, an incredibly successful trader, was telling Bud Fox, an aspiring trader, how he had become so wealthy. He said, "The richest one percent of this country owns half our country's wealth. One-third of that comes from hard work; two-thirds comes from inheritance, interest on interest accumulating from widows and sons, and what I do—stock and real estate speculation."[2]

There it was. My answer. This was my ticket to being rich. It absorbed me. It intrigued me. It fascinated me. Stock speculation. It was everything that I wanted in a career: unlimited potential, unlimited opportunities, and best of all, unlimited riches. The life of a trader was my dream.

After completing graduate school, I had a difficult time getting a job. I wanted to trade stocks; however, no one would let me do it. For two months I exhausted myself and heard repeatedly, "Todd, your resume looks great, but we are just not hiring." I told myself, *I am bright, educated, and have a burning desire to do this. Why don't I start my own business? Yeah,* I thought, *why don't I?*

There was only one problem: no money.

Again, I evaluated why I had gone to school. I went to learn how to think. Thinking was the answer. I then noticed multiple credit card letters scattered across my room. Each one mentioned that they would give me a five thousand dollar credit line with an introductory interest rate of 4.9 percent that would last for six months. The fine print said that after six months the interest rate would increase to 19.8 percent. Yikes! Then the thought hit me: *What if I apply for four credit cards simultaneously? What if I get approved by all four? I will have twenty thousand dollars to begin trading. What if?*

The next thing I knew, I was approved by all four credit card companies and had money to trade. What happened next can be attributed to anything from luck, timing, brilliance, or divine favor. I now believe that God wanted to show me some principles of His kingdom because what took place was remarkable.

After diligent research, I invested in a few companies whose stock skyrocketed. Within six months, the twenty thousand dollars turned into one hundred thousand plus. It was amazing. Here I was, a twenty-four-year-old, making six figures in less than six months. The greatest thing was that I was doing what I loved—trading stocks. As a reward to myself, I went out and traded my Jeep Wrangler for a Mercedes Benz. The difference I paid in cash. Here is where the story takes an interesting turn.

Greed began to consume me. I saw how easy it was to turn twenty thousand dollars into one hundred thousand, and I wanted to turn the one hundred thousand into five hundred thousand. Money became my sole desire. The freedom to buy anything I wanted was intoxicating.

Next, I rolled up my sleeves and immersed myself in research, looking for a company with the potential to make me a millionaire. I didn't find any one company with that much potential, but I found a few that seemed like great prospects. I decided to trade stock options instead of stocks. Big mistake.

Options are the rocket ships of the financial industry. Through leverage, one can make huge amounts of money by picking the right stock, at the right time, and at the right price. I had heard traders in the financial markets refer to the "Fiji trade" in which someone puts up a large amount of money in one trade—and succeeds. Then the trader would take all his friends on a vacation to the Fiji Islands.

Well, I didn't put a large amount of money on one trade. I decided to put *all* my money on this trade. I figured one of two things would happen:

1. Everything would work out wonderfully, I would make about five hundred thousand dollars, and I would take my friends to Fiji.
2. I would go broke and lose everything I had.

Suffice it to say, option number one did not happen.

I went broke. I lost all my money and was completely devastated. I remember crying myself to sleep for about a month, thinking about my foolishness. Next I had to move back home with my parents and begin anew. As you can imagine, from a guy who had just "made it," this was very humbling. Yet, looking at the subtle bright side from this sudden loss, I did realize that placing the trade was rather courageous. By allowing myself to step up to the plate, I was able to swing for the fences. But instead of hitting a home run, I had struck out. The positive note was that I had had a chance to bat. As Victor D'Argent expressed in his book *Uncommon Way to Wealth,* "Financial success, you will find, is a by-product of uncommon behavior, which entails the virtues of leadership that include—as I have said—the courage to face the unknown and risk failure."[3] Boy, had I risked failure all right.

Back home I worked a few jobs and saved every dime I made, hoping to return to the financial markets. Within six months, I saved twenty-five thousand dollars and was ready to return to trading. Again, you can call it luck, great timing, brilliance, or divine favor, but what happened next was as if the abundance of heaven was revealed to me.

It felt as though God reached down and poured His anointing on my investments. All of a sudden, the twenty-five thousand dollars grew to one hundred thousand, which grew to five hundred thousand, which grew to one million. This happened within one year. I was a millionaire at the age of twenty-five! Want to know the first thing I did? I went to Disney World. Seriously. I had always told myself that when I made a million dollars, I would go to Disney World.

Soon afterwards, life became even more amazing. Within six months, I made another million. Within a year, I had become a multimillionaire. Once again, however, here is where the story takes an unexpected turn.

I remembered that when I had first started trading, I thought, *If I make one hundred thousand dollars a year, that would be great.* But you know what? After I had made one hundred thousand dollars, I then wanted to make five hundred thousand. After I had made five hundred thousand, I wanted a million. When I had made a million, I wanted two. And when I had made two, I wanted five. Looking back, it is clear that my hunger for riches was unfulfilling.

The words from Ecclesiastes began to swirl in my head, "Whoever loves money never has money enough; whoever loves wealth is never satisfied with his income" (Eccl. 5:10–11). I was in love and her name was money.

I believed a lie. I believed something that is so commonly taught by the world: if you have more money, then you will have fewer problems. As a millionaire, I wouldn't have to rely on people; I could be more independent. *I am in control,* I thought. Money gave me tremendous freedom to do whatever I wanted. It was all about building my kingdom. I was not dependent on God but upon myself. I had forsaken the first and greatest commandment, which is to love the Lord my God with all my heart, soul, and mind.

Christian writer John Foster says, "The pride of dying rich raises the loudest laugh in hell." I knew what this meant, yet I didn't want to acknowledge it. I didn't want to face the idea that I was taking pride in my riches, I knew full well that when I die, nothing goes with me. My pride made me a fool. I began to think that money could be my comfort. Even with all my educational degrees, I became a fool by expecting money to fulfill many of my desires.

But it didn't matter what I thought about money or being rich. I was about to have the floor pulled out from under me once again.

Over the next two years, I lost 95 percent of my wealth. Just as surely as I had had the Midas touch before, I now had the amazing gift of making things disappear—especially money.

It was horrible. Almost every trade I placed lost money. I lost money at an astonishing rate. A friend asked me how things were going, and I said, "Put it this way. If you put a monkey at the desk next to me and train him to do the exact opposite of whatever I did, he would be the richest ape in the world."

As I will describe in the next chapter, God eventually took me to another country to help me redefine what it means to be rich.

Now, the best answer I have ever heard to the question "What does it mean to be rich?" is by Sir John Marks Templeton. Templeton is a multibillionaire and the founder of Templeton Mutual Funds. He has spent a great part of his life handling and investing large sums of money. When asked about his definition of being rich, he said it could be summed up in just one word—*gratitude.*

He explained that if a person has five dollars to his name and is thankful for that five dollars, he is richer than the person who has five *million* dollars and wants five million more. To Templeton, gratitude is what makes a person rich.

In his book *Discovering the Laws of Life,* Templeton writes that we should develop a spirit of thanksgiving.[5] Each moment holds something for which we can be thankful. We can be thankful for so many simple things—like good health or a sunny day. We can be glad that we are alive and able to breathe clean air and wear dry clothes. When we start thinking of things to be thankful for, our lists can grow and grow: friends, teachers, pastors, schools, libraries, dogs, and cats.

Templeton may be right. Being rich can be defined in one word—*gratitude.*

We find this spirit of gratitude at a place in the Bible where we would least expect it. This quality is displayed in a man who lost everything, a man who was respected by his community and loved by his family. His name is Job, and there is a book in the Bible named after him.

The Bible describes Job as a "blameless and upright man; he feared God and shunned evil" (Job 1:1). It says he was a family man with seven sons and three daughters. He was very wealthy with "seven thousand sheep, three thousand camels, five hundred yoke of oxen, five hundred donkeys, and a large number of servants" (vv. 2–3). The Bible even goes on to say that he was "the greatest man among all the people of the East" (v. 3).

Job had many things that society would deem as signs of wealth. He had a large estate with many herds of livestock. He had a family with ten children. He had a number of servants. He even had the respect of many people in the world. Job was a man of stature. In a moment, however, his whole world would turn upside down.

> One day when Job's sons and daughters were feasting and drinking wine at the oldest brother's house, a messenger came to Job and said, "The oxen were plowing and the donkeys were grazing nearby, and the Sabeans attacked and carried them off. They put the servants to the sword, and I am the only one who has escaped to tell you!" *While he was still speaking,* another messenger came and said, "The fire of God fell from the sky and burned up the sheep and the servants, and I am the only one who has escaped to tell you!" *While he was still speaking,* another messenger came and said, "The Chaldeans formed three raiding parties and swept down on your camels and carried them off. They put the servants to the sword, and I am the only one who has escaped to tell you!" *While he was still speaking,* yet another messenger came and said, "Your sons and daughters were feasting and drinking wine at the oldest brother's house, when suddenly a mighty wind swept in from the desert and struck the four corners of the house. It collapsed on them and they are dead, and I am the only one who has escaped to tell you!" (Job 1:13–19, emphasis mine)

Can you picture this scene? One moment Job has everything, and the world seems fine. The next moment, Job gets news that he has lost his fortune, his servants, and his family. In essence, all he once had is now gone. Everything!

Look at what Job does after hearing this news:

> At this, Job got up and tore his robe and shaved his head. Then he fell to the ground in worship and said: "Naked I came from my mother's womb, and naked I will depart. The Lord gave and the Lord has taken away; may the name of the Lord be praised" (Job 1:20–21).

Notice, even after losing everything, Job realizes the temporal nature of worldly possessions and says, "The Lord gave and the Lord has taken away; may the name of the Lord be praised" (v. 21). Job praises God even though he cannot possibly understand all that is happening. Job recognizes that God is in control even when his life doesn't make sense.

Can we learn to praise God even when we don't understand what is happening? How about you? Whatever stage you are now in, are you able to praise God for the adversity or prosperity you are currently experiencing?

Even amidst the incredible turmoil of realizing that he had lost everything, Job thanked God. Under enormous tribulation, gratitude came from his lips. Job praised God. As wild as it may sound, Job was still a rich man. Why? Because he had praise and gratitude in his heart. What an amazing attitude!

Jesus instructs us to have this kind of attitude when it comes to our money. "Do not store up for yourselves treasures on earth where moth and rust destroy, and where thieves break in and steal. But store up for yourselves treasures in heaven where moth and rust do not destroy, and where thieves do not break in and steal. For where your treasure is, there your heart will be also" (Matt. 6:19–21). Job was thanking God and storing up treasures of praise even in the midst of this bizarre time in his life. He knew that God was still in control.

This is not to downplay any problems that you are currently experiencing. Problems are real. Pain is real. Pain seems to be a necessary part of growth. Oxford scholar C. S. Lewis says, "God whispers in our comfort but shouts in our pain."[6] Often in life we don't know where we are going or how to get there. But the one sure thing we can know is that God loves us and loves it when we seek Him. Following Him is the one constant we need. Jesus reminds us, "I have told you these things, so that in me you may have peace. In this world you will have trouble. But take heart! I have overcome the world" (John 16:33). In this world we will have trouble, but our assurance needs to be focused on God.

"Where your treasure is, there your heart will be also" (Matt. 6:21).

Strive to be rich. Be wealthy. But become so by giving thanks to God for whatever you have. Being rich can be summed up in one word—*gratitude*. If you have gratitude in your heart, it will flow out of your lips and into the lives of others.

As Job said after losing everything, "Naked I came from my mother's womb, and naked I will depart. The Lord gave and the Lord has taken away; may the name of the Lord be praised" (Job 1:21).

Imitate the attitude expressed by Job. First Thessalonians 5:16–18 says, "Be joyful always; pray continually; give thanks in all circumstances, for this is God's will for you in Christ Jesus." Colossians 2:6–7 reads, "So then, just as you received Christ Jesus as Lord, continue to live in him, rooted and built up in him, strengthened in the faith as you were taught, and overflowing with thankfulness."

Jesus talked more about money than any other topic in the New Testament. I'm sure Jesus knew of all the difficult decisions we face when it comes to money. We have so many different options when it comes to how we can spend our money these days.

What if there was some type of filter that would help guide us in all the decisions we face? What if there was a way to keep our focus on God?

In the next chapter, we will look at two priceless words that can guide us along any path that life presents. These two words will allow you to make the right decisions every time. Let us discover these two priceless words.

TWO PRICELESS WORDS

hat if I told you that there is an answer to almost any question you have? What if I told you that this answer is the same for any decision that you are about to make? Would you believe me? Well, I am about to share with you the answer to virtually every question you have about life.

When times are bad, what should you do? When times are good, what then?

If I could present one piece of advice for your future, this would be it: two priceless words. These two words can guide you throughout life. The answer to any question you are facing can be filtered through these two words. These two words are not "pay attention," although this is always important. These two words are not "get ready," although this is also very important. So pay attention and get ready for the two most important words you may ever hear.

The two words that can never steer you wrong are . . . *follow God*. That's it. Two words. Follow God. When in doubt, follow God. When seeking direction, follow God. When life seems upside-down, follow God. When times are good, follow God. When times are bad, follow God.

After I had lost everything financially for the second time, I knew that I needed a break. Losing millions of dollars hurt far

worse than losing a mere one hundred thousand. I needed coun-
seling. I needed to refocus on God, not Todd. Once again, my world
had turned upside down. For two years, I had lived in Chicago
one block off Michigan Avenue in a rather exclusive area appropriately called "The Gold Coast." Now my world was changing fast.

I unplugged from the financial markets and decided to radically change my perspective. A friend suggested that I join him on
a Christian mission trip to Mexico. Our job was to deliver beans,
rice, and Bibles to some of the poorest areas in the country. The
next thing I knew, I was in Mexico. In the blink of an eye, I had
journeyed from the opulence of downtown Chicago to some of the
poorest parts of Mexico.

This trip truly rocked me.

Here I was an overeducated trader from Chicago, delivering
food and Bibles to people who could not even afford a meal. Yet, in
their eyes, I could see dignity amid the poverty. I could see children, unadorned with material wealth, beaming like precious jewels lost among discarded refuse. I saw children that God loved and
wanted to meet. I saw their countenances change after they asked
Jesus into their lives. I saw them radiate a hope that they could not
articulate that was planted deep within their hearts and shining
through their eyes.

In Mexico, God taught me about true riches. I, Todd, a city
boy, virtually broke financially and not understanding where God
was leading, passed along an explanation of the greatest gift ever
given to me—the gospel of Jesus.

It was here that I began to understand the apostle Paul's words
to "fix our eyes not on what is seen, but on what is unseen. For what
is seen is temporary, but what is unseen is eternal" (2 Cor. 4:18).

The Bible contains the secret formula for following God. To
follow Him, we must recognize that He is God and we are not. We
are His children. We learn how to please our heavenly Father by
obeying His commands. To understand His commands it is important to read His book, the Bible.

In chapter four of Matthew, Jesus calls the first disciples. Do
you know what He says to Peter, James, John, and Andrew? He

uses these two precious words, "Follow me." This is the first instruction He gives His followers. They are Jesus' first and continual instructions for each of us as well.

It is interesting that at the beginning of the Bible we see what happens when we follow someone other than God. The first occurrence of this takes place in the Garden of Eden. The two characters are Adam and Eve. The instructions are to enjoy any tree in the garden but not to eat from the tree of knowledge. Guess what happens? Sure enough, Adam and Eve eat from this forbidden tree.

God then asks Adam, "Where are you?" (Gen. 3:9). Adam replies that he is afraid, naked, and hiding. God asks, "Who told you that you were naked?" (v. 11). Uh oh, someone is in trouble. God knew exactly where Adam and Eve were. He wanted them to acknowledge the truth that they had followed someone other than Him.

Let us look at how Adam and Eve got into this mess. Problem #1: They were disobedient. They did not follow God's instruction to refrain from eating from the tree of knowledge. Not following God always leads us into trouble. Problem #2: Since Adam and Eve did not follow God, they were following someone else. Any voice contrary to God's is not good. It is not right. It is not His voice. We must learn to make our decisions based upon what the Lord desires. It is the one filter that guides us to where we should be. Jesus said, "My sheep listen to my voice; I know them, and they follow me" (John 10:27). His voice is the one we must follow.

But how do we know God's voice?

While visiting a monastery in Cambridge, Massachusetts, I asked a very similar question of a monk who had spent over twenty years meditating and listening for God's voice.

I asked, "In all your years of prayer and reflection, how do you differentiate between your voice and the voice of God?"

The monk confessed that this is a common struggle for most people. He then explained how he has learned to hear God's voice. The monk asked me to envision a large orchestra with a maestro standing at the front. He continued by saying, "The maestro looks at the orchestra and motions to the flutist. The flutist comes out of the orchestra. The maestro instructs you and the flutist to go into a separate room.

"While in this room, the flutist shows you his flute. He explains all the different tones and notes that can come from this instrument. The flutist plays the flute and hits the many ranges of sounds. After a considerable amount of time, the maestro motions for you and the flutist to rejoin the group. He then instructs the flutist to go back into the orchestra. The maestro turns to you and says, 'Now, before I begin to conduct the symphony, I want you to listen only for the flute.'"

As the symphony plays, do you think you could hear the flute amid all the other instruments? I bet you could. Such is the same with listening to the voice of God. We must get alone with God to hear His voice. In our times of silence and prayer, we learn to hear His voice, just as we could learn to hear the flute. Then, when the symphony plays, we can recognize the sound of the flute.

We learn to listen to God's voice so that we can follow Him. Often in life we don't know where we are going. You may be getting ready to graduate from school. You might be considering a new job. You may be considering marriage. With your heart tuned to God, you can rest assured that He will lead you.

Contemplative Christian writer and monk Thomas Merton writes in his personal journal:

> My Lord God, I have no idea where I am going. I do not see the road ahead of me. I cannot know for certain where it will end. Nor do I really know myself, and the fact that I think that I am following your will does not mean that I am actually doing so. But I believe that the desire to please you does in fact please you. And I hope I have that desire in all that I am doing. I hope that I will never do anything apart from that desire. And I know that if I do this you will lead me by the right road, though I may know nothing about it. Therefore I will trust you always though I may seem to be lost and in the shadow of death. I will not fear, for you are ever with me, and you will never leave me to face my perils alone.[1]

Jesus' first instructions to "follow Him" are also the continual directions we have throughout life. During His Sermon on the Mount, Jesus said, "But seek first his kingdom and his righteousness, and all these things will be given to you as well. Therefore do not worry about tomorrow, for tomorrow will worry about itself. Each day has enough trouble of its own" (Matt. 6:33–34). The Bible points us in the direction we need to travel. The writer from the Book of Hebrews instructs us to "fix our eyes on Jesus, the author and perfecter of our faith" (Heb. 12:2).

Following God means constantly seeking His guidance. We need to ask God for the things we need; however, God may give us something entirely different than what we ask. This poem titled "Confederate Soldier's Prayer" says it all:

I asked God for strength, that I may achieve;
    I was made weak, that I might learn humbly to obey.
I asked for health, that I might do greater things;
    I was given infirmity, that I might do better things.
I asked for riches, that I might be happy;
    I was given poverty, that I might be wise.
I asked for power, that I might have the praise of men;
    I was given weakness, that I might feel the need of God.
I asked for all things, that I might enjoy life;
    I was given life, that I might enjoy all things.
I got nothing that I asked for, but everything that I had hoped for.
    Almost despite myself, my unspoken prayers were answered.
I am, among all men, most richly blessed.

—ANONYMOUS

Do you believe that God can richly bless you by giving you something entirely different than what you request? God sees the whole picture. He sees all the details of our lives and the world around us. He knows what we need better than we do. That is why it is best to follow Him.

In many instances, we don't believe God. As Chuck Colson stated in his book *Loving God,* we believe in God, but don't believe God.[2] Let me explain. God has given us the Bible. In this book are promises to those that love Him and have been called according to His purpose (Rom. 8:28). When we seek God and follow Him, we learn that the safest place is with our eyes completely fixed on the author and perfecter of this faith, Jesus Christ. He is the way, the truth, and the life (John 14:6). He is God. He is all-knowing, all-powerful, and omnipresent. Best of all, He wants to help you learn to trust Him to take care of all your concerns.

The work of God is to believe in Him. Believe in His words, His promises, His teachings. Believe that God made you. Believe that He made you unique and special. Believe that following Him will take you to places you would have never expected.

We need God in our lives. We should aspire to walk by faith and not by sight; without faith "it is impossible to please God" (Heb. 11:6). God will give you all the resources you need once you start following Him. Sometimes following Him looks different than you would expect, but He will give you all you need to keep focused on Him.

In the previous chapters, we have defined success by living to please God. We have become rich by allowing gratitude to flow from our heart. We can now answer any question we are facing by applying two priceless words: *Follow God.*

Next we are going to look at dreams. You may be thinking, *What does following God have to do with my dreams?* or *Can I follow God and still have dreams?* Great questions.

The next chapter will focus on the secret to your dreams.

chapter four

THE SECRET TO YOUR DREAMS

hat do you want to be when you grow up?" You may have been asked this question many times as a child, quite a few times as a teenager, and even more so as an adult. It's a great question. You may wish you had a great answer.

When I was younger, I wanted to be a fireman. Then I wanted to be an astronaut. Then I realized that I really wanted to be Superman's replacement when he got older. Sure, that sounds silly, but I felt that someone would have to fill his spot once he retires. Who wouldn't want to have X-ray vision and fly?

In college, I didn't find a degree pertaining to super heroes, so I began to think differently about what I would do in life. People began asking me a new but similar question: "After school, what do you want to do with your life?"

It's a question all students consider. What will you do afterwards? Where will you work? What do you enjoy doing? What are your dreams? What are your hopes? What is your place in this world?

Following my trip to Mexico, I revisited all these questions and reconsidered what dreams God had given me. You may want to do the same at this point in your life.

In a true story, a student arrived late to math class, finding two math problems on the board. Assuming this was the weekend's homework, he wrote the problems in his notebook and took them home.

During the weekend, he toiled on the math problems. Finally he completed the first and then the second. On Monday he submitted his work and explained to the teacher that although it had been quite challenging, he had solved the problems.

The teacher was puzzled. "What homework? I did not assign any homework this weekend."

"Sure you did," replied the student, "the two problems you wrote on the board. Wasn't that our homework? They were tough, but I was able to do them both. Here is my assignment."

The teacher froze in awe as he reviewed the work. Then, lifting his eyes to the young man, he said, "Do you know what you have just done?"

The student replied, "Yes, I did the homework."

"No. The two problems that I placed on the board were not this weekend's homework. They were two famous outstanding problems in mathematics that no one has been able to solve. You just solved both of them."[1]

This young man did not know that the problems were supposedly "unsolvable." But what if he had known? Would he have attempted them anyway? What if? What if we didn't impose limitations on what we could achieve? What if we focused on working toward solutions? What if we didn't let people tell us what we could or could not do?

The student from the previous story was attending the University of California at Berkeley while working on his graduate degree in mathematics when he solved these two problems. His name is George Dantzig, who is now a professor emeritus at Stanford University in Palo Alto, California.

Another person who challenged what others deemed as impossible asked himself a "What if" question in the 1950s. What if he could run the mile in less than four minutes? It was considered impossible. No one had ever run the mile in less than four minutes, but this man believed it was possible. Then, on May 6, 1954, he accomplished the "impossible" in front of an unbelieving world. His name was Roger Bannister.

"Unbelievable! Bannister broke the four-minute barrier. Unbelievable!" This was the mantra from the crowd of spectators. Three minutes and fifty-nine point four seconds. Bannister had accomplished the impossible. The difference of six-tenths of a second allowed him to realize a dream. Bannister's extra effort put the world in awe.

Bannister believed in living out his dreams. He also had the strength to act upon his deep convictions. A year later, fifty-seven people broke Bannister's record. The year after that, over three hundred did.[2] What was once considered impossible is now considered possible. Why? Why hadn't these three hundred people broken the record sooner? What if they hadn't imposed limitations on the four-minute mile? What if? What if we didn't let fear or limitations prevent us from doing what others say cannot be done?

We all have talents, skills, and abilities to make a tremendous difference in life, and many times we don't even realize it. Have you ever wondered what your life would be like if you were truly living out your dreams?

Picture your BIG DREAM. The fantasy. The oh-my-gosh-type dream. Now picture a significant step toward making that dream come true. If you desire to be a concert pianist, are you playing the piano each day? If your longing is to be a poet, are you writing poems or presenting your works at local coffeehouses? Do you have a desire to be a minister? Are you currently taking courses in theology? The point is that you need to visualize your dreams and take active steps toward them. Bannister must have thought that breaking the four-minute barrier would be so awesome that he was willing and able to do whatever was necessary to accomplish it. While the world saw impossibilities, he saw what was possible.

Ken Gaub, in his book *Dreams, Plans, Goals*, writes:

Most of us also would like to leave this world having made a positive mark on those around us. Dreamers are the people who accomplish the deeds that history remembers.

The size and scope of our dreams vary, however, as do our motives. Some dreams tend to be selfish; others are selfless. Most of us have both kinds of dreams.

Jesus admonished, "Seek first the kingdom of God, and His righteousness, and all these things shall be added unto you" (Matt. 6:33). If we seek God's will for our lives, our dreams will fall into their proper place.

We, however, have to plan and work to make our dreams happen. We cannot just say, "Whatever is to be will be." We must exert ourselves in an organized way in order to see our dreams come to pass.[3]

I must warn you that when you come to the point of being able to articulate your dreams, strange things can begin to happen. This holds true in almost any endeavor. People are going to oppose you. When you know what you want and set out to attain it, people are going to say outlandish things. Consider these examples:

"How long will you go on training all day in a gymnasium and living in a dream world?"
—ASKED BY ARNOLD SCHWARZENEGGER'S *family* AS HE TRAINED TO BECOME MR. UNIVERSE

"Liquidate this business right now and recoup whatever cash you can. If you don't, you'll end up penniless."
—THE *attorney* FOR MARY KAY ASH BEFORE SHE OPENED HER FIRST STORES

"It's a cutthroat business and you've got no chance of success."
—*Accountant* FOR ESTEE LAUDER, FOUNDER OF A MULTIBILLION-DOLLAR COSMETIC EMPIRE[4]

Now let's look at dreams from a spiritual perspective. Pretend that heaven was handing out job assignments and God said you could choose whatever you would like to do that would give you joy and Him all the glory. What would you choose? Think about that for a moment. Think about what would make you happy and please God. How can you make that happen? What would you do that would result in giving you joy and God all the glory?

Do you remember Beethoven the plumber? How about Dr. Seuss the opera singer? Or Emily Dickinson the tap dancer? No? Of course not! Beethoven composed music. Dr. Seuss (a.k.a. Theodor Geisel) wrote wonderful children's books, and Emily Dickinson astonished the world with her provocative poetry.

The philosopher Abraham Maslow said, "A musician must make music; an artist must paint; a poet must write if they are to be ultimately at peace with themselves. What one can be, one must be." God has designed His children with skills that are unique to them. As King David wrote:

> For you created my inmost being; you knit me together in my mother's womb. I praise you because I am fearfully and wonderfully made; your works are wonderful, I know that full well (Ps. 139:13–14).

David understood that God does not make junk. God makes masterpieces. God made you. God made you unique. You are created by a God who loves you and knows every hair on your head. He designed you for a purpose. The apostle Paul agrees: "For we are God's workmanship, created in Christ Jesus to do good works, which God prepared in advance for us to do" (Eph. 2:10).

What has God dreamed for you? Have you ever asked yourself how your desires to serve and the needs of the world might connect? Have you ever thought about what gifts God has given you?

What comes to mind when you think of Walt Disney, John F. Kennedy, or Martin Luther King Jr.? Dreamers? From the onset, as it was for these people mentioned, when you start pursuing your dreams, people will say you are crazy, and they will openly tell you what you can or cannot do. Can you just imagine Walt Disney going around telling the world that his little hand puppet by the name of Steamboat Willie would appeal to the child inside all of us? Who could have imagined Walt Disney's dream growing so large all because a hand puppet turned into a mouse named Mickey? Some people say that it is quite sad that Walt died and never got to see Disneyland completed. Quite the contrary, it is because he saw it before anyone else did that we now have Disneyland.

John F. Kennedy believed that the United States could put a man on the moon. With his vision, in 1969 NASA did just that. Kennedy's dream of putting a man on the moon became a reality. The great thing was that he could articulate this dream and share this vision with others.

How about Dr. Martin Luther King Jr.? This was a man with a dream. The world seems to be fearful of the person who not only has a dream but also embarks upon achieving it. As King said on August 28, 1963, on the steps of the Lincoln Memorial:

> I have a dream that one day every valley shall be exalted, every hill and mountain shall be made low, the rough places shall be made plain, and the crooked places shall be made straight and the glory of the Lord will be revealed and all flesh shall see it together. This is our hope. This is the faith that I go back to the South with.[5]

Consider the question that we opened this chapter with: What are you going to do with your life?

When we search for answers, it can be a beautiful thing because we begin to ask questions. Questions are wonderful tools. They can act as mirrors reflecting how we see ourselves and can further help us understand how we see this world. I love asking questions, I love discussing questions, and I love listening to the questions of others. Certain questions can change our lives.

Let us look at how a life-changing conversation dramatically affected John Sculley. His story began because someone asked him a powerful question.

The year was 1983. Steve Jobs was one of the founders of Apple Computers; he was instrumental in the release of the Macintosh computer. He and other Apple executives hoped that this computer would be revolutionary. They wanted this computer to help people realize the power to be their best.

Jobs knew that a key ingredient for the success of Apple Computers was a strong marketing campaign. So Apple set out to find the best marketer in the nation. They found John Sculley, the president of Pepsi-Cola at the time. Sculley had no desire to leave his job.

He had all the luxuries one could desire in a job: a thirty-by-twenty-foot office in New York with a private bathroom and nine windows looking over a private garden below, an executive assistant, an annual salary of five hundred thousand dollars, and hundreds of thousands more in stocks and options. Sculley also had a marvelous home in Greenwich, Connecticut, which was nestled on four and one-half acres of land and was personalized with custom floor-to-ceiling windows and three-hundred-pound doors of oak.

Jobs recognized that Sculley would be a great asset to Apple, and he wanted Sculley to be Apple's Chief Executive Officer (CEO). At the same time, Sculley was not willing to leave his current position. Pepsi provided him with a huge office, great pay, and a positive future. Although he was secure with his job at Pepsi, Sculley was intrigued with Jobs' passion and brilliance for the computer industry.

In a meeting, Sculley explained to Jobs that for him to even consider the offer, Apple would have to offer one million dollars in annual salary, one million dollars as a sign-up bonus, and one million dollars in severance if the position fell through.

Jobs replied, "Even if I have to pay for it out of my own pocket, I want you to come to Apple."[6]

Sculley responded by saying that although he would love to be an advisor to Apple, he wanted to stay in New York as opposed to moving to California. This was not acceptable to Jobs, who wanted Apple to have the best employees and wanted Sculley's genius to lead their marketing campaign face to face in California, not over the phone or while commuting from New York.

They were at an impasse. Jobs became frustrated because he knew that Apple's new computer, the Macintosh, was revolutionary.

Finally Jobs stopped the conversation, paused, and stared at the floor before issuing a formidable challenge to Sculley. Then he said it. He asked a question that put everything into perspective. Lifting his eyes and turning toward Sculley, he asked, "Do you want to spend the rest of your life selling sugared water, or do you want a chance to change the world?"[7]

Sculley later commented that this challenge knocked the wind out of him. It made him think seriously about accomplishing exciting things in this world. The thought of selling sugared water versus being a pioneer in the computer industry made him evaluate what he was doing with his life.

Questions can change our lives. Many times questions help us think about what we are doing, how we are living, and what we aspire to do. Selling sugared water or accepting a chance to change the world was a formidable challenge offered to Sculley. The question changed his life and the very fabric of our economy. How about you? Do you want a chance to change the world?

What do you want to do with your life?

You were born, you live, and then you die. How will you be remembered?

What dreams has God dreamed for you?

Have you asked God where your gifts and the needs of this world meet?

Walt Disney—crazy? John F. Kennedy—crazy? How about Steve Jobs or John Sculley? My guess is that there were a lot of people telling them they were crazy when they began to share their dreams.

My story began when I started telling people that I wanted to live my dream of becoming a trader on Wall Street. Surprisingly friends, family, and others said many discouraging things. "You'll never make it." "Trading is for the financial elite." "You won't be able to compete against the professionals." Instead of words of encouragement, I experienced words of doubt and dejection.

How about you? Have you ever had someone call you crazy for sharing your dreams? How about when you share your faith? What usually happens when you share the exclusive claims of Jesus? Jesus said, "I am the way and the truth and the life. No one comes to the Father except through me" (John 14:6). Jesus obviously knew His purpose and was able to articulate why He came into this world. As Jesus said, "For God so loved the world that he gave his one and only Son, that whoever believes in him shall not perish but have eternal life. For God did not send his Son into the world to condemn the world, but to save the world through him" (John 3:16–17). Jesus came to do His Father's will.

Ask yourself these questions. What do you want to do with your life? How are you sharing your gifts with others? What are you doing for God's glory and your pleasure? Dr. Albert Schweitzer said, "The ones among you who will be really happy are those who will have sought and found how to serve."

My hero Superman acknowledged that his talents were not for his own benefit but for the betterment of mankind. As Superman said, "I look upon my powers as a gift, not mine alone but for anyone who needs them."[8] The Bible says, "There are different kinds of gifts, but the same Spirit. There are different kinds of service, but the same Lord. There are different kinds of working, but the same God works all of them in all men" (1 Cor. 12:5–6).

I believe the real Superman of history is Jesus. The great thing is that Jesus has no plans of retirement. He challenges us to imitate Him, not so that we may replace Him, but so that we can assist in establishing His kingdom on earth as it is in heaven. God's desires become our desires when we trust in Him with all our heart, soul, and mind. Dreams are important. Dreams give us hope and purpose.

I believe the secret to our dreams is God. By allowing God to establish our dreams, we can pray for courage and the ability to follow Him wherever He leads. We must be mindful of the things that rob us from courageously following these dreams, however. We need to identify these robbers. Jesus said, "I have come that they may have life, and have it to the full" (John 10:10b). In contrast He said, "The thief comes only to steal and kill and destroy" (v. 10a).

In the next chapter, we will look at what could be the number one robber of your dreams.

chapter five

THE NUMBER ONE ROBBER OF YOUR DREAMS

This was Karl's big break. Finally a cover story that would captivate the masses, intrigue the public, and send his career skyrocketing. For three months, he considered important people to interview: CEOs, political leaders, movie stars, professional athletes? No, this story had to be different. He had to choose someone powerful, someone deliberate, someone firmly focused on his or her tasks.

It came to him. The interviewee he thought of was compelling, mysterious, and passionate about his work. Karl knew that these are the essentials that make great copy. The interview would be with none other than . . . Satan.

Karl immediately began thinking of the premise for this interview. Maybe he would ask Satan how he got started. Maybe he should ask what motivates him. No, these questions were far too common. He needed to present something fresh and provocative. He needed to find out what Satan's greatest weapons are. That was the story Karl wanted to break: Satan's greatest weapons.

The interview took place in the fiery throngs of the devil's home office. Arriving right on schedule, Karl wasted no time in starting the interview. His first question was, "Satan, would you tell me what weapons you use to fight mankind?"

A smirk slid across the devil's face as he gloated with boastful pride. "Weapons? I am the master of defeating people. It is because of my cleverness and my devious focus that I succeed. I am proud of the weapons that assist me in keeping people down. You are a fool to think that you can possibly understand my ingenious strategies. I'll humor you, however, and give you a glimpse of my arsenal."

Karl was led into a giant warehouse with many doors. Stepping toward the first door, Satan turned to face him and with a mean and nasty smirk said, "Behind this first door are some devious weapons. I use them to make people fight against each other. When I get them fighting amongst themselves, I hardly have to do anything except sit back and enjoy the show."

Satan opened the door to a dark room filled with mean and bitter people shouting, "You can't do it! You're a loser! No one will ever like you! You were born to fail! Give it up!" The shouts amid the room were seemingly coming from every direction.

Satan grinned and said, "What they are shouting is one of my favorite toxins—the poison of negativity. I'll place that in the way of a person who is about to do good. Negative power is immense. People quickly tune into this voice and cannot hear the other One. Ha! Just the first of my great weapons!"

He slammed the door and proudly walked down the hall to the next chamber. Karl's mind swelled with remembrances of all the negative voices that had been spoken into his own ears every time he sought to do something good.

Karl noticed earnest pleasure emanating from Satan as he displayed his arsenal. The devil seemed to be delighting in his wickedness, and this made Karl sick.

They approached the next door.

"Behind this door are some of my most innovative weapons. I use them to let people destroy themselves. When I get them to believe that these substances will cure their problems, I hardly have to do a thing except sit back and enjoy the show," Satan declared. He opened the door and the room was filled with all sorts of drugs—cocaine, heroin, marijuana, and alcohol—a whole assortment to choose from.

"I tell people that these things will cure their problems, take away their pain, and give them peace. What lies! Their conditions get worse and worse, and I sit back and watch them deteriorate into lifeless victims." With an evil smirk and one quick motion, Satan slammed the door as he laughed mockingly at Karl.

The devil paused for a moment and then continued to the final room of the warehouse. The door they approached was over fifteen feet high and made of black iron. "In here is my greatest weapon. Getting people to fight amongst themselves with negativity is a clever trick. Making people insecure through drugs is also quite novel. Those weapons pale in comparison to the effectiveness of what's behind this door, however."

Karl's curiosity grew. *What could possibly be more powerful than the previous weapons?* he wondered.

Satan turned toward Karl and bore into him with a nasty stare that made Karl choke on the despair that filled the hallway. Satan smirked as if he had pulled off a terrible crime and had never been caught. Then the devil said, "Behind this door is my greatest weapon." After a long heavy pause, Satan continued. "I use this weapon to have people fight their number one opponent . . . themselves!" He opened the door and the room filled with darkness. "Go in," Satan taunted, "and marvel at my weapon."

The absence of light frightened Karl; he could not see a thing. He heard Satan bellow from the hallway, "There, in the center of the room, is my greatest weapon. Keep walking. You'll see it."

Karl stepped to the center and saw nothing. Then he noticed a small black seed. He picked it up and asked Satan where his greatest weapon was.

"You're holding it," Satan remarked condescendingly.

Karl didn't understand.

"This little black seed is your greatest weapon? I've just seen mean and nasty people shouting lies to fill my mind with negativity. I've seen drugs of all sorts used to keep people down, and you're trying to tell me that this little seed is your greatest weapon?"

"Oh yes," Satan remarked. "That small dark seed is the seed of fear. When I plant that in someone, they make it grow. It feeds on their fears and becomes stronger with doubt, disbelief, and despair. Ooooh, what a marvelous weapon!"

Satan filled himself with pride as he continued, "I love watching people destroy themselves because they're too scared to pursue their dreams, too scared to take risks, too scared to be different, and too scared to trust the promises of God. I enjoy nothing more than to watch people defeat themselves by letting their fear grow stronger than their faith. Ha! My greatest weapon: the seed of fear."

There it is—the number one robber of our dreams. Fear.

We need to look at fear, understand fear, recognize fear. We need to know where it comes from and how it is discussed in the Bible. Satan's weapons attack the mind, body, and spirit. The apostle Paul knew this very fact when he wrote, "For our struggle is not against flesh and blood, but against the rulers, against the authorities, against the powers of this dark world and against the spiritual forces of evil in the heavenly realms" (Eph. 6:12).

Have you ever thought about what kind of spirit God has given you? The answer can be found in the Bible. Second Timothy 1:7 says, "For God hath not given us the spirit of fear; but of power, and of love, and of a sound mind" (KJV).

John Ortberg, assistant pastor of Willow Creek Community Church in Chicago, Illinois, found that the most common command in all the Bible is not to love God, although that is very important. The most common command is not to go and spread the gospel, although that is also important. The most frequent command given in all the Bible is "fear not."[1]

Fear not. The most frequent command.

Do you know what fear does? It paralyzes. It suffocates. With fear controlling our lives, we don't step out of our comfort zones. We don't move. Fear keeps us paralyzed and prevents us from living a life of faith.

Fear is not an attribute of the Spirit of God within us. Yes, we are to be fearful of God but not of life. Nowhere in the Bible will you find God scared of anything. Therefore, as we emulate Jesus, we should exercise that spirit of power, love, and self-discipline.

In the tenth chapter of Matthew, Jesus conveys words of instruction to His disciples who are about to minister to others. In verses 26–32, Jesus tells the disciples three times not to have fear of "them" (people who are without God) but to have fear of "the One who can destroy both soul and body in hell," (that is God):

> So *do not be afraid* of them. There is nothing concealed that will not be disclosed, or hidden that will not be made known. What I tell you in the dark, speak in the daylight; what is whispered in your ear, proclaim from the roofs. *Do not be afraid* of those who kill the body but cannot kill the soul. Rather, *be afraid* of the One who can destroy both soul and body in hell. Are not two sparrows sold for a penny? Yet not one of them will fall to the ground apart from the will of your Father. And even the very hairs of your head are all numbered. *So don't be afraid;* you are worth more than many sparrows. (Emphasis mine)

Psalm 111:10 says, "The fear of the Lord is the beginning of wisdom." Yes, we are to fear God but not man. As David writes in Psalm 27:1, "The Lord is my light and my salvation—whom shall I fear?" With God on your side, there is truly nothing to fear.

There is a force more powerful than fear. It conquers and beats it every time. It is the essence of how we live. It is an essential attribute of Christianity. The one thing that beats fear is faith. Hebrews 11:6 says, "And without faith it is impossible to please God." We need to apply our faith and let God conquer our fears.

First John 4:18 says, "There is no fear in love. But perfect love drives out fear, because fear has to do with punishment. The one who fears is not made perfect in love." By putting faith and love into action, we have a powerful force working within us.

We must actively apply our faith. Faith with works is the ingredient that dissolves fear. "Faith is being sure of what we hope for and certain of what we do not see" (Heb. 11:1). We live by faith and not by sight. Faith pleases God. Faith works. Faith hopes. Faith believes. Faith coupled with works is alive. "Faith without deeds is dead" (James 2:26).

Understand fear, acknowledge it, and then overcome it by applying your faith. Don't let this seed be planted in you and nourished by doubt, disbelief, and despair.

Mark Twain said, "Courage is the resistance to fear, master of fear; not the absence of fear." Fear is always present, but we don't have to serve it; it can serve us. We can be either a slave to our fear or the master of it. To master our fear, we must recognize it in our lives and then keep our focus on following God.

What we focus on tends to grow and expand. If we have fear in our minds, we will gravitate toward affirming those thoughts. This leads to inaction. It paralyzes and suffocates us. Yet, when we replace fear with faith, then power, love, and a sound mind take over. This leads to a life of action and faith with works. We then experience freedom and peace with God, knowing that He is our focus and courage.

I believe fear is the number one robber of our dreams.

Let's review what we have explored thus far:

Success is—living to please God.
Being wealthy can be defined in one word—*gratitude*.
Two magic words that can help you in any situation are—
    Follow God.
The secret to your dreams is—God.
The number one robber of your dreams is—fear.

The next chapter will focus on a new way of looking at life. This will be a 180-degree paradigm shift from that which most of the world promotes.

Let us take a look at what it means to think differently.

chapter six

THINK DIFFERENTLY

This chapter is dedicated to everyone who has read this far. I hope God is challenging you in many areas of your life. Now, get ready, because I have saved the best for last.

First, I stand up and applaud those who want to do something special in life. Life can be difficult; we all know this. However, life gets a bit easier when we understand that we are not alone. God is with us. By acknowledging His presence, we can hear a small voice whispering, "You are precious and honored in my sight" (Isa. 43:4).

To those people who truly want to be alive and to embrace life, this chapter is for you. As Dale Carnegie said, "The biggest lesson I have ever learned is the stupendous importance of what we think. If I knew what you think, I would know what you are, for your thoughts make you what you are. By changing our thoughts, we can change our lives."[1]

As Pastor James Meeks from Salem Baptist Church in Chicago says, "The world will never see how big God is until they see us doing some God-sized things."[2] God can do immeasurably more than we ask or even imagine. He is a big God.

Think about all the promises of God and do something totally crazy: believe them! Actually believe God and take Him at His word. God promises to "meet all your needs according to his glorious riches in Christ Jesus" (Phil. 4:19). He promises to be with you always to the very end of the age (Matt. 28:20). God promises to "work all things for the good of those that love him, who have been called according to his purpose" (Rom. 8:28). These are incredible words of comfort.

With Jesus inside of you, all things are possible! The key principle to remember is that your dreams are for the glory of God. The Presbyterian Catechism states that man's chief end is to "glorify God and enjoy Him forever."[3] I would agree.

I think back over the years and recall many crazy people, ideas, and inventions. One story in particular that comes to mind occurred during the mid-1990s. Apple Computer was counted down and out in the computer industry. The leaders and employees of the company persisted, however, believing the Macintosh was a superior product, and have since re-established the company as a formidable force in the computer industry. Most people said they were crazy. They agreed. At least from the world's standards they were nuts to continue a company that was losing market share and profits.

In 1999, Apple released this T-shirt, appropriately titled "To the Crazy Ones," with this message on the back:

Here's to the crazy ones.
The misfits.
The rebels.
The troublemakers.
The round pegs in the square holes.
The ones who see things differently.

They're not fond of rules.
And they have no respect for the status quo.
You can praise them, disagree with them, quote them, disbelieve them, glorify them or vilify them.
About the only thing you can't do is ignore them.
Because they change things:
They invent.
They imagine.
They heal.

They explore.
They create.
They inspire.
They push the human race forward.

Maybe they have to be crazy.
How else can you stare at an empty canvas and see a work of art?
Or sit in silence and hear a song that's never been written?
Or gaze at a red planet and see a laboratory on wheels?

We make tools for these kinds of people.
Because while some see them as the crazy ones, we see genius.
And it's the people who are crazy enough to think they can change the world, who actually do.
Think different.[4]

I encourage you to think different. Get a little bit crazy. Believe that God made you. Believe that He made you unique and special. Be the person that God designed you to be. Philosopher Henry Moore writes, "The secret to life is to have a task, something you bring everything to, and the most important thing is—it must be something that you cannot possibly do." The things that we are made to do and the things we dream about cannot possibly be accomplished without God directing our lives. We need God in our lives. This is how He gets the glory and we receive the joy of serving Him.

Many people spend all their energy seeking pleasure, power, and recognition. Jesus said that a world of pleasure centered on possessions, position, or power is ultimately worthless. Whatever you have on earth is only temporary; it cannot be exchanged for your soul. If you work hard at getting what you want, you might eventually have a "pleasurable" life, but in the end you will find it hollow and empty. The Bible says, "Whoever loves money never has money enough; whoever loves wealth is never satisfied with his income" (Eccl. 5:10). The question we need to repeatedly ask ourselves is: Am I willing to make the pursuit of God more important than the selfish pursuit of pleasure?[6]

Think of your life with the end in mind. What will be said about your life at its conclusion? When you die, how will you be remembered? What will people say about you at your funeral? What are they saying about you now?

What if you just received a note saying that tomorrow your life will be reviewed in its entirety? Every day that you have lived will be audited to see if you have wasted your days or if you have maximized the time that you have been here on this earth. Would this review bring a huge smile across your face because of how you have used the precious gift of time that God has given you? Or would you sink into immediate depression thinking about how much time you have wasted?

Thomas Edison said, "If we did all the things we were capable of doing, we would literally astound ourselves." Wouldn't it be fun to astonish yourself with the life you live? Each day would be great and full of challenges that would strengthen the mind, body, and spirit.

What if we approached each day with this reverse mind-set? What if we were to live our lives with the end in mind?

Richard Leider, a prominent psychologist, spent decades interviewing senior citizens. He asked them what they have learned from life and what advice they would pass on to younger generations. Remarkably, almost all of these older people said the same three things. In an interview with Alan Webber from *Fast Company* magazine, Richard Leider shares his findings. Here is what senior citizens would do if they had their lives to live over:

> First, they say that if they could live their lives over again, they
> would be more reflective. They got so caught up in the doing,
> they say, that they often lost sight of the meaning. Usually it
> took a crisis for them to look at their lives in perspective and try
> to reestablish the context. Looking back, they wish they had
> stopped at regular intervals to look at the big picture. They also
> sounded a warning: Life picks up speed. The first half of your
> life is about getting prepared and getting established. Then time
> shifts gears. You hit the second half of your life, and everything

moves faster. Days turn into weeks, weeks into months, and all of a sudden, you're 65 years old. Looking back, they say, you realize that time is the most precious currency in life. And as they got older, having time for reflection became even more important.

Second, if they could live their lives over again, they would take more risks. In relationships, they would have been more courageous. And in expressing their creative side, they would have taken more chances. I think it was Oliver Wendell Holmes who said, "Most of us go to our graves with our music still inside us." Many of these people felt that, despite their successes, their music was still inside them. Almost all of them said that they felt most alive when they took risks. Just being busy from business made them numb. Aliveness came with learning, growing, stretching, and exploring.

Third, if they could live their lives over again, they would understand what really gave them fulfillment.[7]

We can learn so much from those who have preceded us. Our parents and grandparents are turning around and saying three things: be more reflective, take more risks, and seek fulfillment. I would add a fourth item to that list: think differently.

Believe in God instead of the world. Believe that God wants you to have a great job and a great purpose that only you, with your unique gifts, can achieve. Many times our gifts can be displayed through our work because work allows us to expose our true potential.

And if we spend most of our life working or getting ready for work, why would we ever do something that we did not enjoy? There is a saying that if you do not love what you do, then you will never do what you love. Henry Drummond said, "You will find as you look back upon your life that the moments when you have truly lived are the moments when you have done things in the spirit of love." What would your life look like if you truly loved your work?

Thomas Garrity, former dean of the Wharton School of Business in Pennsylvania, commented, "Man works for the profitable employment of one's time." We work to obtain a profit. We want a return on our investment of time, talent, and energy. This work usually produces payments in the form of internal and external rewards. An internal reward can be the sheer joy of doing something you love. This is a reward that fills you with peace and a sense of purpose in your life. An external reward would be something similar to money.

Now, allow me to challenge you with a different perspective on money. What if you thought of money as spiritual energy?

Consider how we pour water on seeds to help them grow. By watering seeds, we have the opportunity to assist in their growth. By doing this, we nurture the seeds so that they might live and blossom. Money, just like water, has this same quality. Whatever you apply money to can grow and flourish.

Sherman Smith, a pastor and business scholar, writes, "From my experiences in dealing with people and their finances, I have learned one important lesson: The way money is used determines whether it becomes a curse or a blessing."[8] When we take our money, time, talent, or treasures and share them with a person in need, with the church, or when we perform any act of selfless giving, we are pouring energy into these things and saying "grow and flourish." The opposite also holds true. If we take our money and use it to buy drugs, filth, or unholy things, we are in essence giving energy to these items and saying "grow and flourish."

Someday you and I and everyone on this planet will have to give an account as a caretaker for whatever God has entrusted to us. The constant questions a Christian must ask are: "How much money shall I use for God?" and "How much shall I use for myself?" The main focus needs to be pleasing God. Remember, "For we must all appear before the judgment seat of Christ, that each one may receive what is due him for the things done while in the body, whether good or bad" (2 Cor. 5:10). The Bible also says, "From everyone who has been given much, much will be demanded; and from the one who has been entrusted with much, much more will be asked" (Luke 12:48).

These are powerful statements. God wants us to make careful decisions with our money. God will teach us how to do that as we study the Bible and listen to His voice. We need to realize that we truly own nothing. We can possess much but own nothing. It is all God's, not ours. The Psalmist writes, "The earth is the Lord's, and everything in it, the world, and all who live in it; for he founded it on the seas and established it upon the waters" (Ps. 24:1–2). Thus, we are only stewards of God's creation.

Thinking differently means actually believing God—believing in all His promises found in the Bible. Thinking differently means living your life with the end in mind while risking, reflecting, and seeking fulfillment. Thinking differently means viewing your money as spiritual energy and directing it upon people and things that you want to "grow and flourish."

The next chapter will discuss where we can get the greatest return on our lives, our possessions, and our investments. Where should we invest our lives? With whom should we invest our time? The final chapter will reveal an investment that could be greater than anything you could expect or ever imagine.

chapter seven

YOUR GREATEST INVESTMENT

any philosophers throughout history have encouraged the examined life. The saying of Plato and Socrates was "Know thyself." Taking time to examine your thoughts, your time, and your talents can be a wonderfully rewarding process.

From my own self-examination, I have learned that I am a trader. I am trained and experienced in that field. But now, my definition of success and my dreams have changed. In the poorest parts of Mexico, God taught me what it means to be rich. He taught me that "The LORD sends poverty and wealth; he humbles and he exalts" (1 Sam. 2:7).

The Lord taught me about thankfulness. I saw the gratitude these children had for the food we gave them and the gratitude they had after accepting Jesus' message of a life in which "No eye has seen, no ear has heard, no mind has conceived what God has prepared for those who love him" (1 Cor. 2:9).

Gratitude means knowing that God loves you. It means knowing that He will lead you, guide you, instruct you, and teach you great and unsearchable things if you seek Him with all your heart (Jer. 33:3). Gratitude is a spirit of thankfulness that Jesus died on the cross for your sins, my sins, and the sins of the world.

I have learned that this life is not about establishing my kingdom but about establishing God's. It is His kingdom that shall come. It is about His will being done on earth as it is in heaven. There is an Italian proverb that says, "Once the game is over, the king and the pawn go back into the same box." The more I meditate on this proverb, the more I realize how temporal money and possessions can be.

Now, as I take new risks and reflect on the gifts and talents that God has given me, I believe I have found the "one thing" that brings me complete fulfillment. My one thing is to live a life that glorifies Jesus. I am no longer after results according to the world's standards. I am after obedience to God. I want to live a life that is pleasing to Him.

I am still a trader. I am still an investor. Right now, I am pursuing the Fiji trade of a different kind. In the Parable of the Sower from Matthew 13, Jesus describes how we are to plant seeds. Some of the seeds will fall on rocky places, others on thorns, and others on good soil. "But the one who received the seed that fell on good soil is the man who hears the word and understands it. He produces a crop, yielding a hundred, sixty or thirty times what was sown" (Matt. 13:23).

I am here to plant seeds. I want to trust God and produce a crop yielding a hundred times what is planted. I never know what growth will occur from these plantings of God's Word; but I press on with faith and assurance, knowing that God, who has called me into "fellowship with His Son Jesus Christ, is faithful" (1 Cor. 1:9).

I no longer live to please myself but to please my Lord, my God, my Savior—Jesus Christ.

Having made and lost millions of dollars, I can tell you just one thing. The greatest investment you could ever make is not in this world but in the next. When Jesus said that He has "come so that you may have life, and have it to the full" (John 10:10), He meant now and forever. Your financial situation in life may change. Close friends and people in your life may change. The only constant that never changes is God. "Jesus Christ is the same yesterday and today and forever" (Heb. 13:8).

Jesus Christ is the greatest investment you could ever make.

conclusion

TRUE RICHES!

his book was very difficult for me to write. I wrote it after visiting one of the lowest points in my professional life. After losing millions of dollars, I revisited the question, "What is this life all about?"

By asking this question, I found myself at a major crossroads. I felt like God was speaking and presenting me with a choice. The first option seemed to be that I could go back to the financial markets and use my education, persistence, and experience to make a new pile of money. In my second option, I could follow another road that would allow me to share the story of Jesus around the nation and make other people rich beyond their wildest dreams.

Well, I've chosen option number two. God's love has radically transformed my life. I don't know if I will ever grasp how much God loves me, but I do know that the more I submit my life to His will, the more I have a peace that surpasses all understanding. I further acknowledge that there is nothing I can do to repay God for this gift of salvation that He has freely given me. The Bible says, "For it is by grace you have been saved, through faith—and this not from yourselves, it is the gift of God—not by works, so that no one can boast" (Eph. 2:8–9). I truly have nothing to boast about other than the fact that God loves me.

The more I think about it, the more I believe that the life of following Jesus is a real life fairy tale. Just like any fairy tale, the best part is what happens at the end. The end of this story occurs the moment we die. It is then that we will meet God in heaven. We cannot even comprehend how glorious a place this will be. This fairy tale concludes with God's children spending eternity in heaven with Him.

Remember the stories of Cinderella and Sleeping Beauty? Both ended with the main characters living happily ever after. Those were fairy tales. Those stories were developed through an author's imagination and shared through a creative voice. The story of Jesus Christ is real, however; it is not a fairy tale.

We are all sinners in need of a Savior. The sin in our lives separates us from God. To reestablish this relationship, God sent His Son, Jesus, to be the redeeming sacrifice that reunites us with Him. Jesus died on the cross for the payment of our sins and rose again from the dead. He came to share the good news that "whosoever believes in him shall not perish but have everlasting life" (John 3:16). The Bible continues to say, "God did not send his Son into the world to condemn the world, but to save the world through him. Whoever believes in him is not condemned, but whoever does not believe stands condemned already because he has not believed in the name of God's one and only Son" (John 3:17–18).

That's the good news. Believing in Jesus leads to everlasting life. Now this book would not be complete if I didn't share the bad news as well. Just as heaven is a place so wonderful that it is beyond our imagination, hell is a place so awful that we cannot grasp its unending torment. The Bible says that God has "set eternity in the hearts of men" (Eccl. 3:11). One of two things will happen when you die. You will either spend eternity with God or you will spend eternity separated from Him.

In my opinion, the most radical statement in all of history was made when Jesus said, "I am the way and the truth and the life. No one comes to the Father except through me" (John 14:6). This is an exclusive claim. Jesus is saying there is only one way to God— and it is through Him.

Oxford scholar C. S. Lewis set out to disprove this claim. Lewis ended up proclaiming Jesus as the Son of God after his intense research. In his book *Readings for Meditation and Reflection,* he writes:

> But still—for intellectual honour has sunk very low in our age—I hear someone whimpering on with his question, "Will it help me? Will it make me happy? Do you really think I'd be better if I became a Christian?" Well, if you must have it, my answer is "Yes." But I don't like giving an answer at all at this stage. Here is a door, behind which, according to some people, the secret of the universe is waiting for you. Either that's true, or it isn't. And if it isn't, then what the door really conceals is simply the greatest fraud, the most colossal "sell" on record. Isn't it obviously the job of every man (that is a man and not a rabbit) to try to find out which, and then to devote his full energies wither to serving this tremendous secret or to exposing and destroying this gigantic humbug? Faced with such an issue, can you really remain wholly absorbed in your own blessed "moral development"?[1]

The greatest fraud or absolute truth? What do you think?

In his book *The Jesus I Never Knew,* modern-day scholar Philip Yancey shares the two main reasons why he became a Christian:

1. The lack of good alternatives.
2. Jesus. Brilliant, untamed, tender, creative, slippery, irreducible, paradoxically humble—Jesus stands up to scrutiny. He is who I want my God to be.[2]

Jesus Christ changed this world. As Yancey writes, "You can gauge the size of a ship that has passed out of sight by the huge wake it leaves behind."[3] Jesus left behind quite a wake.

The world encourages people to be rich, to obtain personal fortune, and to establish a kingdom of their own. Jesus taught principles to establish His kingdom on earth as it is in heaven. As Jesus said:

> For whoever wants to save his life will lose it, but whoever loses his life for me and for the gospel will save it. What good is it for

a man to gain the whole world, yet forfeit his soul? Or what can a man give in exchange for his soul? If anyone is ashamed of me and my words in this adulterous and sinful generation, the Son of Man will be ashamed of him when he comes in his Father's glory with the holy angels (Mark 8:35–38).

True riches can be yours. True riches can be found by making Jesus the God of your life and by living to please Him. Your life can have the fairy-tale ending with you living happily ever after as a citizen in the kingdom of heaven. True riches exist in Jesus Christ.

I became a Christian at the age of seventeen. I reflect now on how I have let money steer me away from God. Even as a Christian, I confess to having served money over the Lord. My faith has grown considerably over the years. Now I see how God has given me the ability to make money to serve Him. It's all for His glory, not mine.

I pray for abundance in life and in the lives of others. And yes, I pray for abundance with money. I rest in the comfort knowing that God is in control. "The LORD sends poverty and wealth; he humbles and he exalts" (1 Sam. 2:7). I have experienced both poverty and wealth, and, thank God, I have learned not to trust in things of a temporal nature but to trust in Him. Be mindful of all the different ways God can bless you. As William Hazlitt remarked, "Prosperity is a great teacher; adversity is a greater one. Possession pampers the mind; deprivation trains and strengthens it." Poverty and prosperity can be two tremendous blessings given by God.

I would also encourage you to view your money as spiritual energy. Water the plants that serve God's purpose. Don't serve money, but serve God through your money. Allow God to bring abundant finances into your life by working hard, but always be mindful that it's for His glory, not yours. The Bible clearly says, "No one can serve two masters. Either he will hate the one and love the other, or he will be devoted to the one and despise the other. You cannot serve both God and Money" (Matt. 6:24). Define what you want more than anything else and you have found your master.

Dream the dreams that God has dreamed for you. The most important one He has is for you to spend eternity with Him. Follow Him. "Trust in the Lord with all your heart and lean not on your own understanding" (Prov. 3:5–6). Make it your goal to please Him. Think of your life as playing to an audience of one where the only person you want to get up and give a standing ovation at the end of your life is Jesus. Understand that once you ask Him into your life, He is with you always. Don't fear. God can work all things together for your good and His glory.

Take a moment to think about what you have just read within this book. Consider going to a quiet place to be alone with God and ask Him what dreams He has for you. Listen for the sound of that beautiful flute amid the playing symphony. Ask Him why it is so important to follow Him. Ask God to help you define success and to reveal what it means to be rich and what it means to think differently.

Most importantly, ask God about the greatest investment you could ever make. Ask Him about His Son Jesus. It is God who will unveil your eyes. He will allow you to see. Neither this book nor I will transform your life. Jesus Christ will, if you allow Him.

The story of Jesus Christ is just like the story I shared at the beginning of this book with the two boys. Having heard the message of Jesus is analogous to having precious diamonds in your hand; yet we cannot even comprehend the infinite value. Don't be like the two young boys who traded their jewels for meaningless candy.

Invest your life in something worthwhile, something eternal, something that will reap rewards beyond that which you could ever imagine. Invest your life in true riches. Invest in Jesus Christ.

May you live happily ever after with God in heaven while enjoying His Son, Jesus. This is "an inheritance that can never perish, spoil or fade—kept in heaven for you" (1 Pet. 3:4).

True riches are found in Jesus. May this be the greatest investment you ever make in this life and ever after.

final words

Write to me! If this book has touched your heart or has been a source of inspiration in your life, I would love to know.

You can send letters to:

letters@littorch.com

or write by mail to:

**Lit Torch Publishing
ATTN: Letters
PO Box 5264
Santa Cruz, CA 95063**

Also, I am available to deliver presentations and seminars at your school, place of business or church. Visit www.littorch.com for more details.

May God be the true source of wealth in your life and may He lead you into paths of righteousness for His name's sake.

Living now and investing forever,

about the author

Broke at 23. A millionaire at 24. A multi-millionaire at 25. Practically broke again at 28. While working as a professional trader in the financial markets, Todd Sinelli lost everything he had and then rebuilt his success multiple times before the age of 30.

Lean in to hear the stories of Mr. Sinelli's misguided ambition to become rich and relish in the wisdom that he has learned about the secret to success, having dreams, and the greatest investment you could ever make.

Todd A. Sinelli holds a bachelor of business degree in marketing from Michigan State University, and an MBA degree in business management from the University of Dallas. Todd holds a number of advanced degrees including: Certified Fund Specialist (CFS), Accredited Asset Management Specialist (AAMS) and has completed the Certified Financial Planner (CFP) course. He has also studied at The Wharton School's Executive Education Program.

Experiential and academic education have been driving forces in Todd's life. His new ambition is to educate others about the difference between material and spiritual wealth through the challenging message contained within *True Riches*. He can be reached at www.littorch.com.

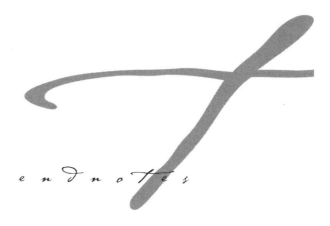

endnotes

Introduction
1. James Kitchens, *Talking with Ducks* (New York, NY: Fireside, 1994), 14.

Chapter 1: What Is Success?
1. Gerard Smith, *Celebrating Success* (Deerfield Beach, FL: Health Communications, 1997), 1.
2. Ibid., 7.
3. Ibid., 14.
4. Ibid., 35.
5. Ibid., 157.
6. In the original Hebrew language of the Old Testament, the word for *sin*, *chata'*, literally translates into "missing the mark."
7. *City Slickers*, Castle Rock Entertainment, 1991.
8. Dr. James Dobson, *What Wives Wish Their Husbands Knew about Women* (Wheaton, IL: Living Books, 1975), 108.

Chapter 2: How to Always Be Rich
1. Ron Blue, *Master Your Money* (Nashville, TN: Thomas Nelson, 1997), 19.
2. *Wall Street,* Twentieth Century Fox, 1987.
3. Victor D'Argent, *Uncommon Way to Wealth* (Dublin, Ireland: Charterhouse Publishing, 1994), 57.
4. John Marks Templeton, *Discovering the Laws of Life* (New York, NY: Continuum, 1994), 13.
5. *Shadowlands,* Savoy Pictures, 1993.

Chapter 3: Two Priceless Words
1. Thomas Merton, *Thoughts in Solitude* (New York, NY: Farrar, Straus and Giroux, 1958), 79.
2. Chuck Colson, *Loving God* (Grand Rapids, MI: Zondervan, 1987), 75.

Chapter 4: The Secret to Your Dreams
1. Cynthia Kersey, *Unstoppable* (Naperville, IL: Sourcebooks, 1998), 117.
2. Ken Gaub, *Dreams, Plans, Goals* (Green Forest, AR: New Leaf Press, 1993), 48.
3. Ibid., 18.
4. Kersey, 140.
5. Jim Haskins, *I Have a Dream* (Brookfield, CT: Millbrook Press, 1992), 79.
6. John Sculley, *Odyssey* (New York, NY: Harper & Row, 1987), 90.
7. Ibid.
8. Alex Ross & Paul Dini, *Superman: Peace on Earth* (New York, NY: DC Comics, 1999).

Chapter 5: The Number One Robber of Your Dreams
1. John Ortberg, *No Fear–Part #1,* audiotape of lecture (Chicago, IL: Willow Creek Community Church, August 7, 1999).

Chapter 6: Think Differently
1. Dale Carnegie, *The Quick & Easy Way to Effective Public Speaking* (New York, NY: Pocket Books, 1962), 25.
2. James Meeks, *Secret of Success,* audiotape of lecture (Chicago, IL: Salem Baptist Church of Chicago, January 6, 1999).
3. Morton H. Smith, *Shorter Catechism of the Westminster Confession Standards* (Escondido, CA: Ephesians Four Group, 1999).
4. T-shirt text (Cupertino, CA: Apple Computer Store, 1999).
5. *Life Application Notes, Mark 8:36,* (Wheaton, IL: Tyndale House Publishers, 1991).
6. Alan M. Webber, *Fast Company Magazine,* 13 (February 1998): 114.
7. Sherman Smith, *Exploding the Doomsday Money Myth* (Nashville, TN: Thomas Nelson, 1994), 207.

Conclusion: True Riches!
1. C. S. Lewis, *Readings for Meditation and Reflection* (New York, NY: Walker and Company, 1998), 15.
2. Philip Yancey, *The Jesus I Never Knew* (Grand Rapids, MI: Zondervan, 1995), 265.
3. Ibid., 17.

To order additional copies of

visit

LIT TORCH PUBLISHING

www.littorch.com